Leaf Manifesto

Laurel Radzieski

Leaf Manifesto
© 2025, Laurel Radzieski

Reproduction of selections from this book, for non-commercial personal or educational purposes, is permitted and encouraged, provided the Author, Book Title and Publisher are acknowledged in the reproduction. Reproduction for sale, rent, or other use involving financial transaction is prohibited except by permission of the Author and Publisher. The exception would be in the case of brief quotations embodied in the critical articles or reviews and pages where permission is specifically granted by the publisher or author.

Books may be purchased in quantity and/or special sales by contacting the publisher. All inquiries related to such matters should be addressed to:

Middle Creek Publishing & Audio 9161
Pueblo Mountain Park Road Beulah, CO
81023
middlecreekpublishing@outlook.com
(719) 369-9050

First Paperback Edition, 2025
ISBN: 9781957483382

Cover Art: Sarah Proctor Perdew.
Interior Artwork: Sarah Proctor Perdew.
Cover Design: David Anthony Martin, Middle Creek Publishing & Audio.
Author Image: Steve Johnson.

Leaf Manifesto

Laurel Radzieski

Middle Creek Publishing & Audio
Beulah, CO USA

Table of Contents

Seed 9
Germination 13
Sprout 27
Seedling 35
Sapling 55
Tree 71
Flowering 97
Fruit 109

For Ryn

Seed

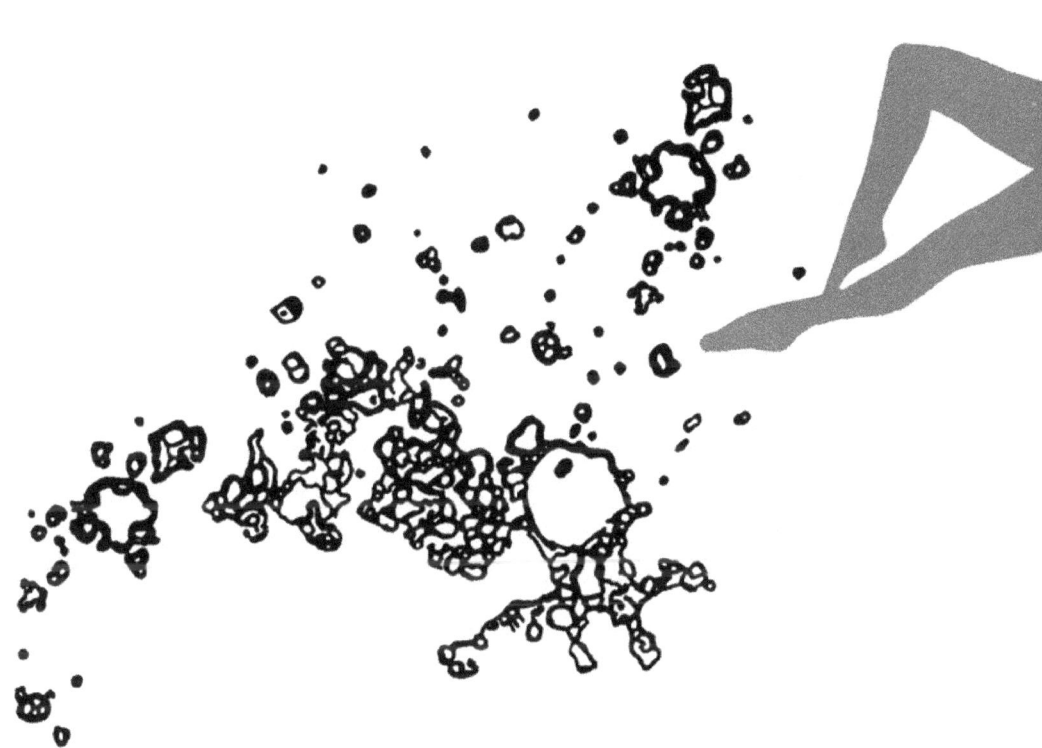

One day I said aloud
I might like to be a tree.

I was uncertain and underprepared.
There were no instructions,

only advisements.
I decided to handle

all seeming directions
infrequently and with caution.

Every day was a bag of old stones
anyway, already sucked clean, all used up.

Bright light pained,
as did dim and the dark.

I tried to become a rock
but was not able.

Tried to become a chair,
a barn, a red clay bowl.

Insects, a hunk of cheese,
another sun, a hill.

I tried being animals.
Tried to be mountains,

caves, a lake.
I tried not changing,

tried staying the same.
But at the end I was still.

(a woman)

Germination

Q: What is a woman?

   A) Some people are born women
      but are not.

   B) Others are not born woman
      but are.

   C) Many born women
      stay that way.

   D) These days loads of people
      sit the whole thing out.

Q: Who gets to be a woman?

    A) Being a woman is a curse.
       Some people carry that burden

       for the rest. Everyone has burdens.
       Being a woman isn't that hard.

    B) No one wants to be a woman.
       So old-fashioned these days.

       Women require too much upkeep,
       too many accessories.

    C) Women are fiction.
       They're in a lot of fairy tales.

       Maybe there used to be women
       but not anymore.

    D) Anyone can be a woman.
       This is upsetting to some people.

       It can be hard to understand
       other viewpoints, other women.

Q: What use is a woman?

    A) Bar the door.
       Stand guard,

       talons out
       forever.

    B) If necessary,
       cut the

       children down
       with an ax.

       (to spare them
       other horrors)

    C) Perhaps womanhood
       is about folds,

       folding or
       unbuckling,

       a particular way
       of falling apart.

    D) A vessel is meant
       to be filled

       or at least
       look pretty.

Women can be tended.
Bend their supple branches

carefully, this way then that.
Teach the reaching limbs

appropriate paths,
discourage poor posture.

Use firm, frequent pressure.

                Some
              feel the call
            to treehood or
          else an aversion
              to green at
              an early age.
              I had no such
            clarity. Trees were
          prevalent by then.
          Bursts of foliage,
            all around, loud
            light seeking –
        for years I beelined
        in the other direction,
         twisting into undergrowth
        away from a life I thought best
      left for later. Then all my friends
    started, settling down, becoming trees
      they had always planned to become, but
  the thought of putting down roots in a secure
  lawn didn't excite me. I tore myself up for not
  wanting that kind of life. I understood the draw,
    mourned the tree I wouldn't become. No one
          wanted to talk about pain of this sort,
                hardly pain,
                more yearn
               in waves, low
              into my   belly,
              all the   time,
               I can   not
                for   give
                my   self
                for   not
               need   ing
               more   of
              life.

As a woman, I am
accustomed to being underfoot/
underneath/underworld.

Many generations of women
dirtied themselves
to heave out of a deeper hole.

Today women get to do work
they want to do as well as
work others do not want to do.

Women have never had it
so good.

Most life started in the mud, then crawling.
     ○ True   ○ False

Trunk and branch are relational to torso and lifted limb.
     ○ True   ○ False

Living is constant contortion.
     ○ True   ○ False

Q: What's it like to be a woman?

    A) Stuff the hole with cloth or cotton.

    B) Insert orange rinds (apply pressure),
       dried herbs. (be gentle)

    C) Try a Ziploc bag, a Dixie Cup, fine china,
       containers to be emptied and rinsed.

    D) Maybe newspaper or wax.

As a woman,
I like to be called.
(like a dog)

As a woman, I am
responsible for tending
the happiness of everyone.

As a woman,
I am tedious
and bizarre.

It's confusing to be
a woman

now that there aren't women
anymore.

Much better to be a tree.
There are still lots of those.

※ ❦ ※

The trend of women turning into trees is not a modern-day phenomenon.
　　○ True　　○ False

Treehood is an evolutionary conclusion,
a yes and both.
　　○ True　　○ False

The lack of recognition that the majority of worker
ants and bees are shes is yet one more
demonstration of the undervaluing of women's work.
　　○ True　　○ False

As a woman,
my indulgence in gender
sometimes requires
external participation.

Women are dull
moss-covered things,
eventually emptied out.

They burn up
from within,
until hollow
all the way down.

Women learn by example.
My mother taught me by
impersonating a dog.

She picked up a piece of meat
from the floor with her mouth,
then refused to share.

Most days I only play
at being a women.

I cannot muster grace, only
lather, spread, kneel.

Even plucking
fails to hide my true self.

I thought my woman
self would be wispy,
reed-like, yet instead I grew

more jagged rock,
more mossy pit.

No blushed swelling,
only heavy heavy
barely standing stone.

So selfish and naïve
expecting otherwise.

I will sleep in this
hole. (I deserve this)

I have disappointed everyone I have ever loved.
    ◯ True   ◯ False

This does not impact my day-to-day life.
    ◯ True   ◯ False

But it could.
    ◯ True   ◯ False

Must a woman be
vessel/object filled?

Always soft servant/
nanny/nurse/cook/slut?

Even an empty snag tree
is of use

unlike me and my pig head/
beetle back/split seed self.

At these times,
above all, I wanted
to be a tree,
as so many others
before me had
or tried to be.
I desired soft petals.

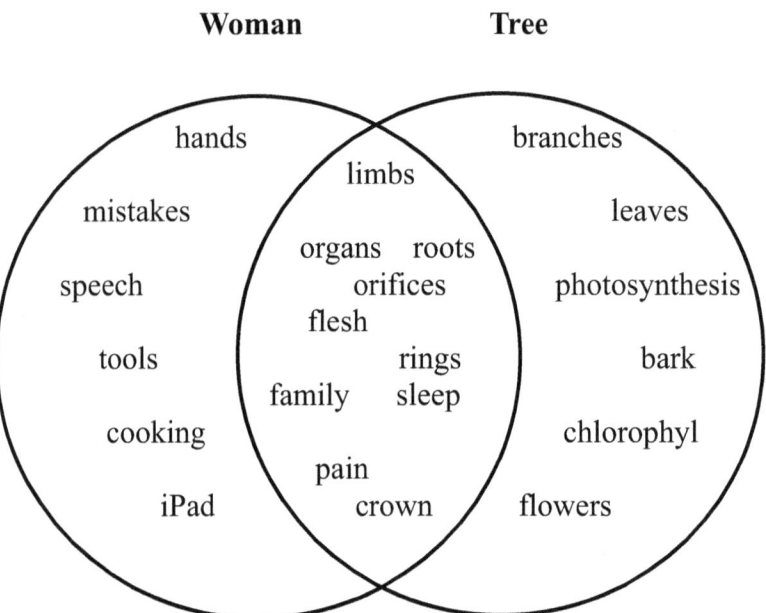

Sprout

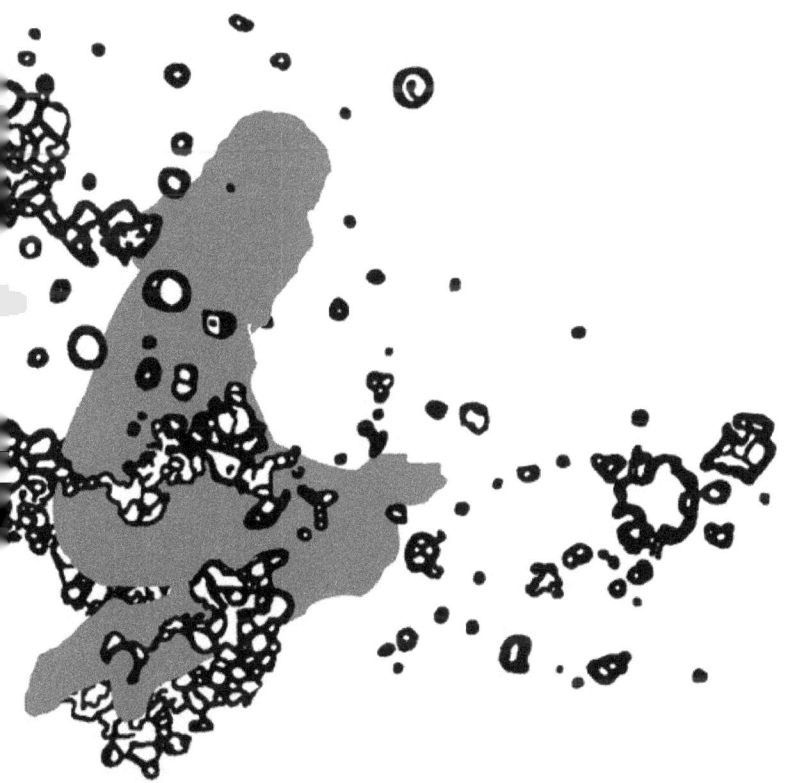

Women are always weeping.
Some women blame others singularly/

completely for personal lacking.
This wounds all women.

Trees lack guilt and blame.
Much better to be a tree.

Nothing bad has ever
happened to me.
      ◯ True   ◯ False

I have no claim to any
inheritance of pain.
      ◯ True   ◯ False

None of my ancestors
were forced to drink
from a trough.
      ◯ True   ◯ False

Being a woman
has never been
so good.
      ◯ True   ◯ False

Some days I think
myself an abomination,

though, truthfully,
I'm not that interesting.

Romanticizing otherness
takes many forms.

Even monstering appeals
in certain circles.

Women are dangerous.
Best cross to the other side of the street

when one or several of them are near.
Women don't have any friends

except for other women.
Women are the worst, always red-faced.
Even when sleeping they frown.

Past Life Regression

Frond of curly moss
I cannot blink, mind as field,
only thirst, grey light.

Q: Do women deserve to be trees?

A: I have been given much
    still been ungrateful, cravenly so.

    I belong in the dirt
    yet sit on a shelf.

    I have never known hunger,
    never earned a soft bed.

    Even as a shared responsibility,
    cultivated with concerted effort

    I sour to curd.
    Don't mind me.

    My words are soiled rags
    meant to be thrown away.

೩ ❦ ೬

I am a forest
despite flapping collar,
my plastic shoes.
I belong in oaky mud.

If I were better at living, things would be easier, but I'm not. That's why this level of difficulty persists.

    ◯ True   ◯ False

Nothing bad has ever happened to me.

    ◯ True   ◯ False

Now I am dreaming in leaves.

    ◯ True   ◯ False

I assumed I was drowning before, but it's worse now.

    ◯ True   ◯ False

Some days everything feels like an affront, even the spiny stems of grapes.

    ◯ True   ◯ False

I am bitten up, diseased.
Insides punched through.

Used up/hollowed out.
Cut down.

I am in pieces
all over the floor/ground/plate.

I had never been singularly concentrated,
never pure woman,
always unclean and wanting.

But nothing bad
has ever happened to me.

Nothing has ever
happened to me.

Repeated admonishment of self is yet another indulgence.
My hands are so dirty, I may as well cut them off.

I have never had to prove my worth
on a mountain or to the rain.

I don't even carry a shield
to hide my face and neck.

Unfortunately, I have
opened my mouth

much too frequently
to be of use to anyone.

I am spiral grasping.
Perhaps if I were smarter/
braver/stronger/more clever,
life would be better.

But I'm not
so it's not.
      ◯ True   ◯ False

Having exhausted
all other options,
I decided to become a tree.

It required resourcefulness,
also selfishness, honesty,
a low sodium diet.

Considering this endeavor, I felt
more alive
than before.

For the first time
I had a goal that didn't
stem from shame.

Seedling

Q: What are the possibilities of treehood?

   A) Everyone will like you. (everyone who likes trees)

   B) You will feel more at peace in the natural world.

   C) You will feel more at peace when not in the natural world.

   D) You will be part of the solution.

How to Identify as a Tree

Consider what others would want to know about your bark patterns and inner rings.

Be prepared to describe your roots and family tree.

Try adding your tree identity to online profiles and email signatures.

If you are on unseeded land, know the history of the ground, how it got that way.

Q: Will being a tree make me taller? I want/don't want to be taller.

A: No – People who turn into trees don't usually have physical height increases, although some report experiencing an elevated visual perspective.

⊰✿⊱

Q: Will being a tree increase my longevity?

A: Maybe – Tree-life and tree-death experiences can vary greatly and may be uncomfortable to discuss with family members. Consider reviewing the average lifespan of an assortment of tree species, noting that median ages often do not reflect the human-turned-tree experience.

Helpful Wellness Tips for Women Who Have Turned into Trees

Do remember that conifer needles clog pipes.
Consider investing in a quality mesh cover to guard
sink and shower drains.

Don't be afraid to go a few months between prunings.
Over-clipped branches appear shorn in daylight.

Do pick cosmetics to complement your bark and complexion.
Try Carbon Capture lip stain, a deep red with chocolate tones.

Don't overwork or over-supplement your soil.
Till and fertilize seasonally to encourage long, healthy roots.

Q: If I turn into a tree, what can I give birth to?

A) Potatoes in a paper bag

B) All types of melons and gourds

C) One large jar of assorted buttons

D) A deflated volleyball

E) Another tree (maybe)

F) Seven pairs of balled up socks tied together with string

G) A chicken, a trout, baby mice

H) Maracas

Q: Can being a tree induce a period in persons who do not experience menstruation?

A: No – There is no scientific evidence to support this claim despite the rampant repetition of the sentiment on social media and many pro-tree, pre-tree and post-tree websites, blogs, and podcasts. These sources purport treehood, particularly related to certain species of trees, can induce a rhythmed menses aligned with the phases of the moon. No peer-reviewed study has occurred to support this claim. Some proponents confirm that a physical bleed cannot be induced through treehood but believe a similarly paced spiritual cycle can be fostered.

Q: Who gets to be a tree?

A: Residency location and economic status are the primary indicators of treehood access. Turning into a tree can be costly and visiting a facility may require extensive planning and travel. Some organizations that appear to offer human to-tree services may actually focus on convincing the individual not to become a tree.

Reputable tree unification centers will not demand a reason or explanation for your decision to turn tree. Adult women should not need signature permission from a spouse or other family member or be required to participate in reeducation in order to seek treehood services.

Plan your tree unification journey early and consult your arborist as needed with questions, noting that local laws may restrict what the professional can say when speaking about treehood options.

Family tree legislation aimed at reducing treehood is common in regions where trees are considered a hinderance to workforce development/the nuclear family/national security.

It's not enough to only say
one wants to be a tree.

There are other ways
to show allegiance.

Try to find a way of conveying conviction,
forethought and investment,

perhaps with a hat
or tastefully placed tattoo.

Demonstrate daily there is nothing
else you'd rather be doing.

These activities will provide
a sling of visible truth.

Q: Do all women want to be trees?

A: The possibilities of treehood
do not appeal to all women.

Each woman is her own
self with unique needs,
desires, and inherited suffering.

Some women back away,
cannot think of a tree
without also a rope.

For these women,
womanhood is often harder
than it is for other women.

Q: Can I still get sick/diseased as a tree?

A: Yes – Trees are susceptible to a variety of diseases and ailments. Good hygiene and regular health maintenance coupled with routine check-ups at your local garden center are the best ways to keep your tree self healthy and strong. After prevention, early detection is vital to addressing health issues as they arise.

Know the Signs of Common Tree Diseases

Infestation: A highly contagious disease that features other organisms subsisting within the individual in a detrimental manner. Common symptoms include the sensation of skin crawling, lesions on or under bark and branches, hearing gnawing, dreams about being eaten, and feelings of being hollowed out or hunted. If infestation is suspected, quarantine immediately and seek an exterminator. Keep away from others, especially small children, elderly adults, and pets.

Q: Why choose treehood?

A: Nothing bad has ever happened to me.
   Still, I am let alone to live

   without destruction or harm
   me and my gravel voice, my long tongue.

   Someday I will be found out
   pinned with a tack to a display board

   nowhere to hide
   from one true corpse.

   Until then, I will no longer pretend
   to be a patient, forgiving soul,
   an unhungry, unbanked sprig.

   It's time to admit I am more
   than a rock that can talk.

   I love you is the sounds of a heavy stone
   dragged across another stone.

In the absence of stress, we do not get to evolve.

○ True   ○ False

Drowning does not require submersion.

○ True   ○ False

No one deserves to keep track of this much paperwork.

○ True   ○ False

One does not need to reach capacity to be too full.

○ True   ○ False

Sometimes people go down to the underworld and come back as trees. It's not a popular method but there are recorded instances.

○ True   ○ False

One day
I said aloud
that I might
like to be
a tree.
To know the
flush of leaning sun,
joy of thick limbs, to be
a burden of sweet round
fruit. I wanted this as one
wants a pet, so embarked on
a path obscured, marked only
by the occasional footprint
etched in late morning.
And the first time I
forgot hunger, nobody
noticed, as if a sad guest
at the wedding quiet crept
from the hall. Life felt much
better for the lacking. Then my
feet sank into soil. Now building
off the roots of others, picking up
where they left off, is easier than
seeking new territories. Before
finding this trail, my days full
of frantic searches, always
digging for the newest
moments, a series of
*Stop here as I taste this
apricot.* Now, I can walk
slowly, talk among the green
mosses and ferns, asking *How
were things before how they are?*
It's not a new idea, gathering
light, watching the moon
grow   wide.

Q: What happens next?

    A) The sun opens.

    B) A monstering performative gesture.

    C) Some of the footprints turn into a pack of wolves. (in the dark)

    D) A storm of trees.

Q: Will treehood help with my arthritis/scoliosis/osteoporosis/hives?

A: Treehood is a tool, only one part of a balanced life.

J.R.R. Tolkien's urge to write what would become *The Lord of the Rings* was initially an interest in answering the question of what would need to occur for the trees to go to war.

    ◯ True   ◯ False

Q: But what if I turn into a tree
   then don't want to be a tree anymore?

A: Surveys show low rates of regret
   after turning into a tree.

   However, in rare instances, persons develop
   disassociation with tree life.

   This can be painful for the individual,
   family and friends. If contemplating

   treehood, discuss post-human scenarios
   with loved ones, ideally early on.

Q: Will being a tree prevent cancer/illness/bad blood?

A: While all organisms are vulnerable to corruption, plant cells differ from those of animals. Imagine a brick wall. While individual sections of the wall crumble, the offending blocks are not sent down a river to other sections of the wall.

Consider the fusion of bone and flesh into one long trunk.

Past Life Regression

Fungi on a toenail,
like broken glass, I'm inside
squirming this deep home.

To be a
tree today is
a political act.
It didn't used
to be, but
here we
are. Highways
now forests of anti-
trunk bumper stickers.
*Friends Don't Let Friends
Go Green! If I Wanted Bark
I'd Get A Dog. Mother Nat-
ure Should Take A Hike!!
Better Keep Your Leaves
Out of My Backyard.*
When I finally voiced
my want to turn   tree
I thought loved   ones
would be happy for me.
Did not expect jokes,
so many questions.
Supportive friends
wanted a schedule.
Dismayed family
saw the lack of
preparation as
indication of my
hesitance. To share
my unplanned desire
loosed floods of confusion
red pain that ravaged my home.
It was a hard, deeply embarrassed
time. Wounded, I gathered my feral
(jagged) self, shut inwards. Practiced
how to appear small (locked) so my
germinating treehood stayed hidden,
went to the office and showed up for
birthday parties, did dishes, rooted in
damp dirt where no one could see or fear.
(interfere) I waited to be born,
to be new.

Q: Is treehood patriotic?

A: The trees of today
   are hope for tomorrow,

   but remember, a forest
   never burned
   lacks practice at survival.

   In other words, the plant
   world is also violent,
   finitely resourced.

Q: Can my being a tree harm others?

A: While individual treehood does not physically hurt others, uncomfortable or painful emotional reactions often occur. Consider how you would feel if a loved one or acquaintance explained that they were other than how you thought. Feelings of confusion, anger, loss, mourning, distrust, betrayal, apprehension, and nostalgia are common.

A: Trees native to your home or origins are often the easiest unifications, as they are more likely to be accustomed to the local ecosystem. However, many cultures, religions and peoples have physical, intellectual, and spiritual ties to trees worth considering. When selecting a species, consider if the tree is sacred to you or others.

A: While a tree may be native to the area and not linked to another culture's sacred traditions, consider the environmental status of the tree within your region.
Is it endangered? Prone to disease?
High maintenance? Odorous?

Questions to Consider when Turning into a Tree

Q: Could unification with this tree have the potential to negatively impact individuals from traditionally marginalized groups?

Q: Could unification with this tree affect others whose religious, spiritual or cultural traditions require access to the tree?

Q: Could unification with this tree contribute to its decline or the decline of an ecosystem?

Q: Are the tree unification components confirmed to be ethically sourced?

Q: What leaf shape will show off my assets?

Q: Who is your favorite famous tree?

A) The Tree of Knowledge

B) The Tree of Life

C) The Giving Tree

D) The Burning Bush

E) The Whomping Willow

F) The Bodhi Tree

G) The World Tree

H) The Tree that grows in Brooklyn

Q: If I turn into a tree will I have access to the same levels of medical care and treatment?

A: Sometimes – Trees are often unrepresented or underrepresented in studies and clinical trials, thus access to medications and health services may be limited. The shortage of healthcare professionals with experience treating tree patients is a widespread challenge.

Know the Signs of Common Tree Diseases

Root Rot: A degenerative disease that disenfranchises the individual from a family or social group with which one was previously associated. Treatments range from simple conversation composting to long-term amputation of family tree limbs. Root rot is typically easier to address if caught at an early stage.

Dating Profile Dos and Don'ts for Women Who Have Turned into Trees

Do use a real, recent picture.
It's okay if your photo doesn't look like it's straight out of Better Homes and Gardens.

Do be specific.
Tall birch looking for taller birch to settle down with.

Do show off your personality and interests.
Loves camping, hiking, and scary movies about deforestation.

Do be open to trying new things.
Unfamiliar with acorns and pine cones but willing to learn. ;)

Don't leave any profile section blank.
Want to know my leaf type? DM me!

Don't exaggerate accomplishments or try to sell something.
~~After years of searching, I found a 100% guaranteed way to get rid of root rot once and for all. Try my method risk free.~~

Don't be afraid to state your boundaries.
Up for enjoying organic fertilizers every now and then but no Miracle-Gro. Not into GMOs.

Q: I'm interested in becoming a Eucalyptus tree but heard that I would be a fire hazard. Are there any safety concerns I should be aware of?

A: Eucalyptus trees are most known for their scent and flammability. Some offices and apartments won't consider Eucalyptus workers or tenants due to the risk they pose to others. There isn't precedent for a Eucalyptus tree being held responsible for deaths in a fire but this may be due to the lack of Eucalyptus trees surviving such a tragedy on record. While species such as Rainbow Eucalyptus are visually appealing, most experts recommend refraining from becoming a tree of this type, particularly if you live with children or enjoy candlelight.

Know the Signs of Common Tree Diseases

Snow White Syndrome: A communicable disease that causes the individual to become highly attractive to animals. Seek medical attention if you believe you are being followed by chipmunks, squirrels, voles, sparrows, robins, blue jays, deer, antelope, or wild boar.

Q: How do I talk to children about trees?

A: Nature crafts and seed planting activities can help get the conversation started. Consider having multiple short conversations in safe spaces where the child can talk freely. Be prepared to listen and answer questions.

Q: What is more appealing, branches or antlers?

Q: What can I do to alleviate my fear of getting chopped down?

Q: What does it feel like to photosynthesize?

Q: Is turning into a tree a lifestyle trend or a movement towards an alternative mode of human existence?

Q: Is being a tree this lonely?

Some nights
I wake afraid,

fearing the seedless
watermelon's plight:

Bulky, tough-skinned.
Intentionally barren.

Needlessly sweet.
(thoughtless)

I am a many lobed _____. Scraping towards and through, concrete to tree.

    A) beast

    B) vessel

    C) flora

    D) soul

    E) machine

    F) undeserving desert

    G) (none of the above)

                            ❧

Having exhausted all other options, I grew a thick, dirty exterior.

    Q: What were the other options?

Turning tree is a subversion of chronological demands, a necessary perversion of society's linear tendencies.

⭘ True ⭘ False

I don't know how to be alive without running myself to ribbons.

⭘ True ⭘ False

Having exhausted all other options,
I decided to become a tree.

It took two years to grow
roots and branches.

Then all seasons were work.

Flowering in spring required my entire focus.
I was unable to cook or clean,

missed birthdays and parties.
The laundry piled unfolded.

In summer my limbs were heavier,
I was even busier.

Fall, an abomination of overtime.
Winter, a slumbering

quiet relief
yet also work.

Even in sleep,
only parts of me rested.

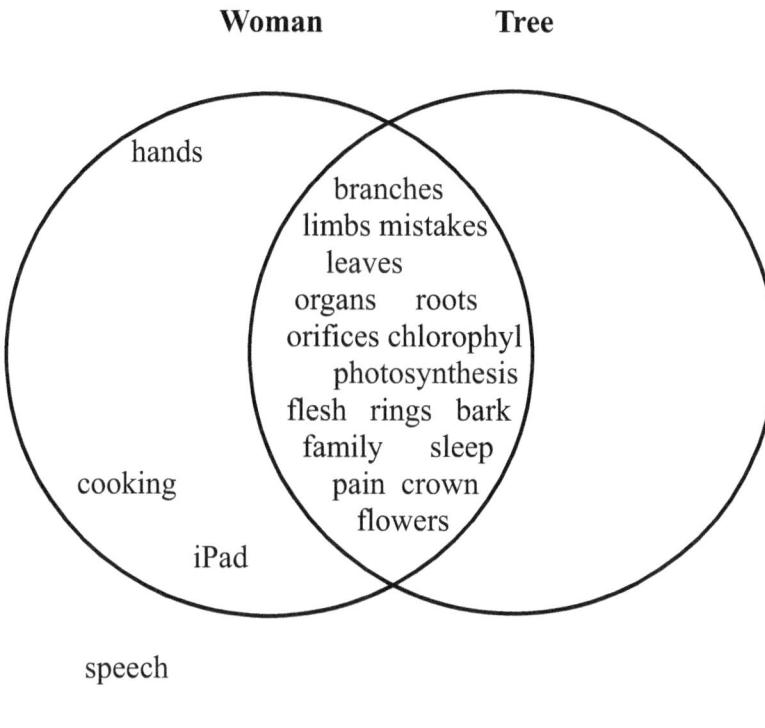

Tree

Affirmations to Add to Daily Tree Routines

"I'm budding because I'm good at it."

"I'm an explosion of foliage."

"I get to flower how I want to."

"I'm chlorophyl reimagined."

"I'm pollinating like nobody's business."

Q: Will turning into a tree help or alleviate my depression/anxiety/seasonal allergies/infertility/anger management issues/addiction/fear of heights/body dysmorphia/eczema/color blindness/FOMO/restless leg syndrome/overactive thyroid/sleeplessness/jealousy of a person who is very dear to me/dry mouth/tinnitus/athlete's foot/bad dreams/fear of the dark/unattractive laugh?

Q: What should I do if I don't want my loved ones to also turn into trees?

A: Modeling is key.
Many trees choose not to engage other trees

in conversation citing they are too self-congratulatory
for most tastes.

If you don't want your children to talk to trees,
don't let them see you talking to trees.

Try to be a positive example of humanity's perks.
Enforce strict no-twigs policy at the dinner table.

When social situations or business transactions require
engaging with trees, be the bigger person.

Speak up if leaf displays or exposed root balls
make you feel uncomfortable.

We're all in this together.

Q: I'm interested in becoming an aspen in order to create an army of linked clone replications of myself.
Is this frowned upon?

A: Reputable clinics and garden centers will discourage customers from turning into any tree possessing capacity for self-duplication. Engaging in unification procedures with such trees is illegal and punishable by up to $100,000 fine and 10 years in prison. Individual attempts to become such species may result in destabilized unification,
injury, and death.

Q: If I turn into a tree, will I still be susceptible to the negative effects of coming in contact with poison ivy/poison sumac/wild turnip/that relative whose disapproval I have a difficult time being okay with?

Q: Is paper murder?

Q: Can my pet become a tree too? I think my dog/cat/hamster/fish/parrot/exotic snake wants to be a tree.

Having exhausted all other options,
I buried my feet and became a tree.

The sound of a dropped bowl
shattering was how my mother
howled when she discovered
what I had done.

Q: Which of the following most closely reflects your opinion of childhood?

    A) I had an upsetting childhood.

    B) I was not often upset during childhood.

    C) I don't remember my childhood.

    D) I didn't have a childhood.

Q: What was it like to be a woman?

A: I followed my father's shadow
into the mountain,
though he did not ask me to.

He went first for, in many cases,
I am slow and heavy.

The mountain climbed
into the sky, unlike me
my damp and shadow.

When my father died
we sawed off his antlers
and tied them above the door

to make our house larger
than the other houses.

Q: What was it like to be a woman?

A: My shame stemmed
from one of my mother's

　　disapproving looks
　　for a choice I had made.

　　She thought I had done
　　the wrong thing in a wrong

　　way and, as a result, irrevocably
　　harmed her.

　　It took several years
　　for me to understand

　　her grief and anger fueled
　　our survival. (made me what I am)

Q: Should I be worried if I develop a burl/many burls? What if my burls change shape/color/size?

A: Not usually – Burls can happen to anyone and are rarely dangerous. Causes may include environmental stresses, traumas (physical/emotional/mental), infection or disease.

A burl is typically not a problem in itself but may indicate a condition or psychic wound worth examining.

Q: What are my obligations (if any) to pollinators?

Q: Which would you rather be?

    A) Undamaged but unremarkable.

    B) Remarkable but damaged.

Despite setbacks –
frontal foliage loss,

irregular rain patterns,
caterpillars,

I began to walk with more ease,
less hunch, more rustle,

less interest in satisfying
the moralities of others.

*Please stop watering me
with that bottled water,* I asked.

*I am living
a different kind of life.*

Q: What type of relationship do you want to have with your fungus companion?

   A) Business partnership

   B) Mutual friendship

   C) Spouses/Lovers

   D) Court appointed representative

   E) Pet and owner (self as owner)

   F) Pet and owner (self as pet)

How To Join a Fungal Network

Place the warm net of not-flesh on a hand.
Admire it.

Feel the web breathing,
faint tickle at the wrist,
sighing.

Gentle probing,
then embrace.

Nothing bad has ever happened to me.
Bad has never happened to me.

My arm is branching night,
noisy blooming light.

Nothing bad has ever happened to me.
Nothing has ever happened to me.

Green expansion,
crusting over, within.

Nothing has happened.
Nothing has ever happened.

I am dreaming of the sky.
My eyes are made of stars.

I cannot see the sky,
so there is no sky.

           When I was
         a woman, I was
         often portrayed as
         crawling. There are
          other things I was
       good at that required
       getting on my knees.
    I knew filth, dragged
    the rag of my body
    underneath and behind
     rehearsed topographies.
     My home was the floor.
      I slept in a little nest of bright
       scraps found in the quiet dirt.
         Women are stray dogs in a dull
          landscape of lint, dust and hair, so
       empty. I shudder   to count how
       many times I ate   my own words,
        whining at some door with chin slopping.
         That's what it was like – wild scratched
          at the doorknob unable to remember
             if I was trying to get in or out.

A: Then it was cold.

It was cold because
my feet angered the ground.

In extreme temperatures,
the body may rattle,
a jar of dried beans.

Then sudden dark,

not as if
my eyes had closed

but rather, as if
I no longer had eyes.

Amongst the swimming green
breath began to slip.

Until this point, I had considered
continuation assumed.

Limping away with a story
cradled in chest, now less certain.

It was at this time I also recognized I was missing
an arm/limb/branch/piece of me.

Recall the crunch/snap of my arm/branch/limb
detached/ripped/torn off.

It went like this. I had my arm/branch/limb,
then I did not.

Yellow pus shot out from the hole,
then steam.

Smoke/burning/cracking wood.
Oh, and screams. (my wail)

☙ ❧

Sometimes a person dies but it takes a few years or even decades for reality to catch up. The same is true for being born.
    ◯ True   ◯

Or maybe the experience was more akin to that time my mother died, how I howled in a parking lot but no one heard me so even this never actually happened.
    ◯   ◯ False

It's too late for acceptance now.
Though a parade, too long,

is wending in the distance,
small trumpets blaring.
Also too late.

Time ran out and I'm sorry.
There's nothing left and I'm sorry.

Tell me about damage,
attempting to bloom
in snowy despair.

About pushing
everything that exists out,

nothing left to do
but wither, turn white then grey.

I am covered in algae.
I am a dumb rock
all alone in a once woods.

◯   ◯

Every day now only a terrible story tumbling from this mouth. I am bare, disgorged loss, perched atop a blade of grass, form outstretched, waiting to be held, willing to embed for rescue. And this part of my self becoming larger than the others.

○   ○

Q: What was it like?

   A) Death was ankles and feet sticking out of a compost heap.

   B) Kicking for days.

   C) The smell was awful.

   D) I do not remember anything about anyone else who was in the room when it happened.

   E) My hands were burned by how it happened. (these are the scars)

I am struck down,
sheared into pieces
on the ground

or is this the floor?
It is dark here, hard-
cold on cheek.

There is no light here.
No friendship here.
Soot in mouth here.

Unlike sleep here.

Q:

A: Now I am crawling. So many items once essential long ago abandoned. (left behind: manilla envelope bulged with life and death certificates, social security card, passport, photo copies of licenses and insurance cards, all lost to the dirt)

Tripping, dropping
clawing.
Unfeeling
hand/feet.

A: Now I am crawling, ground made vertical. Grasping high grass where stalks meet mud. Body pulled along by one-arm dream.

A: I try to drag myself up the wall but my single arm is a shaking, flabby twig. My climbing up this wall is a fantasy I act out in my head as I try and fail. In my mind's eye I have already reached the top of the stonework and am looking for the best way to drop down the other side, but truly I am not a woman. I am not a tree. I am on the ground, scrambled and falling to bits with loss, flailing on my stomach, now back, infant again. This is not productive struggle or a road bump or an incident to rally my spirits, no brace and leap. This moment is a coffin.

A woman is meant to crawl.

That's why she carries
one lung and her intestines
in a handbag.

When a tree/woman falls
she/it/they becomes a gift/offering/tunnel

for others to use and build from.

Women exist
but being a tree is necessary work.
      ◯ Tree   ◯ Woman

A: When I decided to try to climb the wall again I was so unhappy. I stood by lifting my rear, then carefully stacking my back as a child does with blocks, and, also like a child, I was clumsy and tumbled to the ground. Tried again, fell again. Failing to scale the wall was the hardest thing I'd ever done. It took up miles and days. The word "pathetic" was unhelpful yet echoed.

Crawling. (again)
When will this end?

There's a crowning of the hill
nestled at the edge of the sky

as if the green waves are curling up
for sleep.

Q: Having spent extensive time, effort and limbs climbing to the summit, I was heaving, bent over with hand on knee, when the flames arrived. I looked up but the figure was too bright. I only saw a sun that said, "What took you so long?" Every bit of me became a petal.

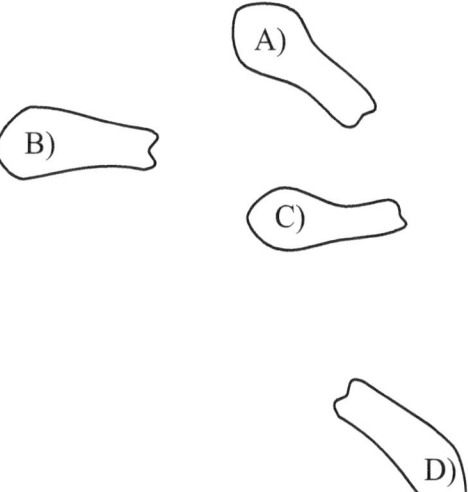

Flowering

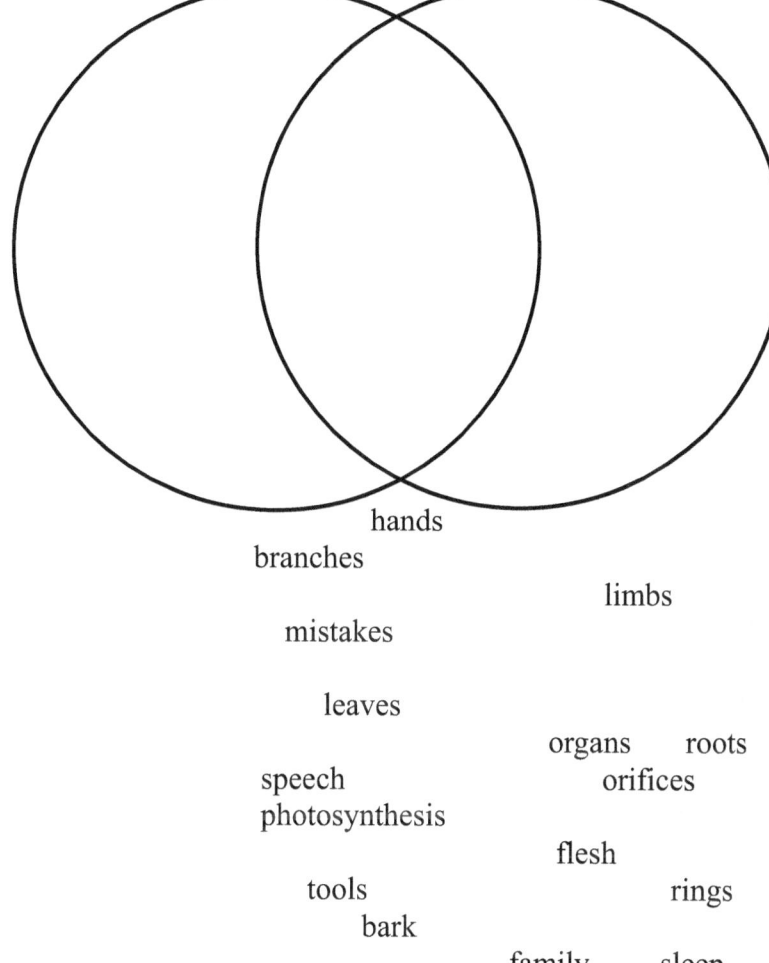

                    hands
          branches
                                    limbs
               mistakes

            leaves
                          organs   roots
          speech   orifices
          photosynthesis
                            flesh
            tools   rings
              bark
                        family   sleep
            cooking

        chlorophyl
                           pain
               iPad   crown
        flowers

I awoke in the garden
with a thin black and white scarf
pillowing my head.

Asking around didn't help.
No one recalled
who I belonged to

or why I wanted to be
somewhere/someone/something
other than I had been.

Q: What happened to me?

Q: Why am I here?

Q: Why am I like this?

Q: How else could I be?

Having wandered here, I could not find my way out.
The gate I had entered through was now an apricot tree.

Q: Is this home?

Q: Is it what I wanted?

Q: Must I always be how I always have been?

The garden was a bore. I sat on a park bench for 12 days, though the days seemed longer than that. My arm-less side was sore but barely so.

◈

This place was not my home. I remembered this locked room.

Though I had lived in a garden, once happily, now again, this time filled with spite and sadness.

Perhaps the sun/sky was right. This was not my garden. Nothing had ever been mine.

Still, I built a nest and lived. But it was not my home.

And, despite deserving otherwise, as is often the case, I was extremely fortunate.

Before I fully understood
the loss of an arm,

it started
to grow back.

I didn't make peace
with anything or anyone,

yet healed anyway.
Even in foolishness,

my actions were
without consequence.
I sat at the bench a long time. No one approached.

I spoke to myself and the trees, the grass, the lazy-headed blue-blue flowers, myself, the trees again, the dirt,

befriended the skies.

Of course, there was more than the bench, yet I stayed, too long. I stayed, even though I recognized this locked/shut room. Door but not a door. In the end, it had always been a solid walled hope, this discovery that was not new. Nothing had not been about getting here/out/in.

Q: What is marcescence?

A: Marcescence occurs when a tree holds onto dead leaves.
Such grasping is not usually indicative of a fatal condition.

To be awake in a time of extended trauma, one's life
serves as an engaged reaction to open wounds.

To be a tree when others are not requires reckoning,
dancing, adjacent denial of death.

The act of letting go is necessary work.
Such tasks are best not left at the door or tied to a pole.

Trees provide hands-on demonstrations of death's
non-obliteration. Plus, a tree is truly they, veiny systems

maintained through shared labor.
A leaf manifesto may reveal the necessity of periodic

release, repetitive freefall, eventual flowers.

An act can be meaningful without being explicit.
One misstep is unlikely to undo every previous effort.

To become a tree is to welcome the fruit of replicable
modeling. Also, green is slimming.

Today could be about being an interesting person,
connecting at the hip. Or talking about plants again.

A title for this lesson could be: The Progression of
Human Yearning for Reintegration with Nature.

Short Answer: Define marcescence as it relates to your life and existence. Use examples from the text or personal experience.

Q: But isn't a tree by default, hierarchical? Isn't such branching another way to keep static structures firm and present?

Only then was it obvious I had been here before.

Not just once, but many times over repeated visitations
swallowed to hazy memory, belated recognitions.

I did not know this soil, this ornate hedge,
this marigold, this quilt on fence, this

seashell bird bath, this mud,
but I recognized the locked room.

Fruit

One day I stood and began down a tan dirt path. The walking swung my body, as did the breeze.

Despite vulnerability and danger,
me and my new head
walked among the pines.

The way through already
etched and paid for.

The day was a golden drop
ready to be pulled down
at all costs.

Others waded these weeds
before me and did so better
with more efficiency and care.

I picked my way through
a seeming trail.

Not original or interesting
yet each sight was still new.

One would think
I'd known the way
by now.

True honesty would be
admitting I have never really tried.

I may never be ready
to hold such failure in this cupped chest.

Instead, let me walk through
my green rain dusk song.

Let me rise before dawn,
try again.

A: And I understand now. The lock, the absence of a door, all this fruit. But at the time the air was buzzing deeply with honeysuckle.

A: So many problems trace back to my wanting to hear myself sound clever.

Q: Why did I venture returning to such a place with so much sweet rot?

A: (Yet another demonstration of my inadequacy/incompetence/lacking/stunted nature/cloven feet/too small breasts/suffering)

Soon the foliage grew denser, wilder,
less trimmed arboretum, more trail damp

trail into deepening woods.
The trees pressed in, against me,

path narrowed, vision blurred.
(I began to fall)

Then when all was certainly lost –

A: The canopy crashed open.
   Cracking rush of light.

   Not a dream.

   And oh! So many trees!
   And people and trees

   who may have once been people and people
   turning into trees.

   All were here,
   a slickened crowd of foliage/flesh intertwined/pulsing/fruit.

It has been so long since hunger,
yet here an apricot hanging,

outstretched branch offering.
Sweet flesh, hazy soft.

I bite first by nibbling the chin.
Lick sweet sap from my palms.

I am ready
to eat/be eaten.

I am ready
to be filled.

Q: Explain it to me –

A: Deep in the woods,
   fern brushes inner thigh.
   Lightning flashes brightly.

Q: Explain it to me –

A: In heaven, everyone gets to be
how they want to be,
even women.

But I knew I was not in heaven
because none of us
had ever died.

Past Life Regression

Fallen walnut. Such
a long way down, but then
soft idea of grass.

Gratitude & Notes

Portions of the text were inspired by engagement with *Leg Art* by Madison S. Lacy and Don Morgan published by Citadel Press.

Reimagined images of famous paintings were created using Wikipedia public domain image resources and Pixabay public domain images.

Thank you to the editorial teams of publications that published pieces of this text, often in earlier forms: Binghamton Poetry Project's online anthology, *Clockhouse, Down the Dog Hole: 11 Poets on Northeast Pennsylvania* published by Nightshade Press, *The New York Quarterly, The Plume, Stained: an anthology of writing about menstruation* published by Querencia Press, Wormfarm Institute's *The Stalk Report, Strike While the Ink is Hot Zine #2* published by But Whole Press, and *Witcraft*. I am grateful to Wormfarm Institute and Lacawac Sanctuary for providing natural settings and space to write.

I am indebted to the organizations whose workshops and classes supported my writing: Art School, Belladonna* School for Feminist Practice & Poetics, The Center for Book Arts, Clockhouse Writers' Conference, and Two Trees Writers' Collaborative. Thank you to my teachers, especially Kate Laster and Elena Georgiou.

Thanks also to Alvernia University, GoggleWorks Center for the Arts, and Berks Bards.

Thank you to the individuals who provided feedback and support.

Special thanks to David and Carolyn Elliott, Sarah Proctor Perdew, Amanda J. Bradley, Daryl Fanelli, and Abby Frankfurt.

Notable thanks to David A. Martin for believing in this book. Thank you to my husband, Michael, for coming with me through the woods. Thank you to my parents, especially my mother, Kristina, for understanding.

About the Author

Laurel Radzieski is a poet and the author of two books, *Leaf Manifesto*, winner of Middle Creek Publishing & Audio's 2024 Halcyon Award, and *Red Mother* (NYQ Books, 2018), a love story told from the perspective of a parasite that won the 2020 Whirling Prize in Poetry from Etchings Press. Her poems have appeared in *Clockhouse*, *Rust + Moth*, *The New York Quarterly*, *Atlas and Alice*, *House of Zolo's Journal of Speculative Literature*, and elsewhere, including on a street sign and roadsides in Wisconsin. She earned her MFA at Goddard College and has been a writer-in-residence at Wormfarm Institute. Laurel enjoys writing poems for strangers in community spaces. She lives in Reading, Pennsylvania and writes at GoggleWorks Center for the Arts. When not writing poems, Laurel is the Director of Grants at Alvernia University. She enjoys playing board games that take up the whole table.

About the Press

Middle Creek Publishing & Audio is a company seeking to make the world a better place through both the means and ends of publishing. We are publishers of quality literature in any genre from authors and artists, both seasoned and those who are undiscovered or under-valued, or under-represented, with a great interest in works which illuminate or embody any aspect of contemplative Human Ecology, defined as the relationship between humans and their natural, social, and built environments.

Middle Creek Publishing & Audio's particular interest in Human Ecology is meant to clarify an aspect of the quality in the works we will consider for publication and as a guide to those considering submitting work to us. Our interest is in publishing works which illuminate the human experience through words, story or other content that connects us to each other, our environment, our history, and our potential deeply and more consciously.

> In 2025, we created a nonprofit, Middle Creek Press, an NTEE A33: Arts, Culture, and Humanities - Printing and Publishing nonprofit organization. We are in the process of transitioning all work and processes over. This change will empower us to focus more on the quality of our work and extend our literary reach. Be part of this transformative journey by supporting our fundraising efforts. Any contribution helps.

If you have a moment, drop us a line at:

editor@middlecreekpublishing.com to give us feedback on our impact that we can use in grants reporting.

www.ingramcontent.com/pod-product-compliance
Lightning Source LLC
Chambersburg PA
CBHW070334180426
43196CB00050B/2635